THE LAWS OF HUMAN PROGRESS AND MODERN REFORMS.

A LECTURE

DELIVERED BEFORE THE

MERCANTILE LIBRARY ASSOCIATION

OF THE

City of New-York.

BY

REV. ORVILLE DEWEY.

NEW-YORK:
C. S. FRANCIS & COMPANY, 252 BROADWAY.
BOSTON: CROSBY & NICHOLS.
M.DCCC.LII.

JOHN F. TROW, PRINTER,
49 Ann-st., New-York.

LECTURE

ON THE LAWS OF HUMAN PROGRESS AND MODERN REFORM.

A discourse was delivered and printed a year or two since, by a distinguished citizen, "on the Law of human progress." The principal object of that discourse, or oration, was to show that progress is a law of humanity. The history of this great idea, the certainty of its realization, and the folly of any conservatism that resists it, were the matters mainly treated of. The *Laws* of human progress; the necessary conditions on which it depends; the forces and the limitations to which all progress, all reform, is subject—this is a different theme; and it is the one to which I propose to invite your attention this evening. I hardly know what subject that I could name, deserves at the present time more attention, or gains less. Or gains less, I say. Declamation enough we have about progress, but very little of the deeper thought that comes from a profound acquaintance with human nature and life and history. We want a *philosophy* of progress, and among all our philosophies, do not seem to have it. I do not now remember a book with this title, the Philosophy of Progress, or the Philosophy of Reforms. If there be none, the want of it is somewhat significant. But the subject equally deserves attention. For the one matter of controversy, that is now rife and raging through the whole sphere of civilization—from the farthest bounds of Europe, from the Bosphorus and the Black Sea, across the whole world, to the coasts of Oregon and California, is *progress*. Restraint and freedom; legitimacy and liberty; Monarchy and Republic; aristocracy and radicalism; conservatism and ultraism—communism, socialism, reform, penal code, private right—the people's rights, the laborer's rights, women's rights, every body's rights, and every body's wrongs—and how to carry on society by some great stride to the righting of all wrongs—these are subjects with which the whole world is embroiled. Indications of every sort, conflicts, controversies, conventions, revolutions, battles, one or other, attest every where the presence of this disturbing element—the desire of progress, of change, of something better, or of what is thought to be better. But it seems to me quite remarkable how rare it is to meet with any book, any pamphlet, any manifesto, any string of resolutions, or any speech in Convention, that goes back to original principles—that goes down to the very grounds of the questions thus agitated, or in other words, to the laws of reason and wisdom which are entitled to settle them. I say the questions; for always there is a question. Ought this to be, or not? Ought nations to choose their own rulers, and ought the suffrage to be universal? Ought the present system of property and the relations of capital and labor to continue, or to be broken up, and society to be reorganized and placed upon a new basis? Ought standing armies to be maintained, or ought they to be disbanded, and nations, on no account nor occasion, to contend with deadly weapons? Ought we to give up our old national policy, and resort to armed intervention in foreign quarrels? Ought capital punishment to be abolished? Ought the slaves to be immediately emancipated? Ought women to have the same education, business, political franchises and public offices, as men?

The common method of discussing these, and many other questions of a like nature, is to espouse one side or the other, and to see what can be said for it. Most writers and speakers are found in the ranks of conservatives or ultraists, and their arguments, while they delight their own party, tend very little to convince the other—perhaps are not even read by the other. Would it not be a better method of proceeding to inquire for the *principles* by which all such questions are to be decided? Might not such a method lead to the discovery, that there is commonly something right on *both* sides, and in some cases that there is a *medium*, which is nearer to the truth than either?

I do not say that any principles can be laid down by which the matters in question shall be immediately or definitely settled. The interests and duties of a multitude of human beings are involved; and such subjects do not admit of any very prompt and clear decision. But certainly the right principles will have some tendency, and may yield some help, to lead us to the right conclusion. Let us then see if we can ascertain what are the Laws, or some of the Laws of Progress; and I pray your attention to this brief discussion, if it shall appear somewhat abstract; for we shall soon have occasion to to apply it to matters that are practical enough. Progress, let it be observed, is of two kinds—inward and outward; of the mind and of institutions. Most questions arise with regard to the latter; and I might confine my view to this. But as they stand closely related—related in fact as cause and effect; as all outward comes from inward movement, and is, in fact, its expression, its symbol, I shall consider them together—discriminating them only as I shall find occasion.

The laws of progress then, come under three general heads: the nature of man; his condition, *i. e.*, in the material world; and his social, including his political relations.

The first law of progress, therefore, is moral freedom. Call this man's birthright or not—*say* or *deny* that all men are born to be free,—one thing is certain, there cannot be one step in human progress without this condition. And it is only from what is inevitably left of freedom to the very serf and slave, that he makes any progress. More in fact is left, than we always consider, or than our current language always admits. Free will, free thought, may be in many ways injuriously checked; but it cannot be extinguished in any human being; if it were, it would be, not slavery, but death to him as a man. And as far as any institution, any authority, any religion, any government crushes down this freedom, its stops the growth of men and communities.

The second law of progress is individual responsibility. The order of nature and providence is, that every man shall answer for himself. The system of the world is a system of rewards and punishments. They are indispensable stimulants to action. Any institution then, monastic, communist, or co-operative, that relieves a man of self-care and personal responsibility, will be fatal to human progress, or in other words, so far as it goes that way, it will have that effect.

A third law of progress is, that it is experimental; wrought out in the mind and experience of men. The truth is, men will not learn in any other way; perhaps they cannot. What is verified in ourselves, is true; all else is dogma, phraseology, not faith. You cannot theorize, legislate, or organize men into an improved condition; they must experiment themselves into it. I do not mean by this, to object to theories, plans, projects; but their proper office is to lead men to try them, and nothing but trial can prove them to be true. And if they go very far beyond the minds they propose to benefit—taking them *out* of the range of fair experiment; if any State organizations or constitutions do this, they must be pronounced visionary, unsafe, and impracticable. With regard to political organizations, our South American States found it to be so; republics could not flourish on their soil; and in the extending popularity of this kind of government, their example of failure is not likely to be the last. It is just as if you should take savages from their rude and filthy huts, and place them in a model village, laid out, arranged, and furnished by all the arts of civilization; they could neither use nor enjoy it, but would throw all back into disorder, and disarray, and filth; they would turn all the fine cottages and villas into huts and cabins again, from which they must again build up and work up their own way anew.

And, therefore, I confidently lay down as a fourth law of progress, that it must be gradual. Little by little does man learn; slowly does he advance; and there is no other way. I need not enlarge upon this point; the matter speaks plainly enough for itself: experimenting is, from the very nature of the case, slow: the onward steps of men are by centuries. It is a law, wisely ordained too; it makes progress thorough; it engages in it the energy and fidelity of men; it makes the advancing steps safe and sure. It makes the result cost something, and therefore makes it worth something. If you were carried to the top of a mountain, by a foreign force, in a moment's flight, you would not value the elevation as you do when you have yourself toiled slowly up the ascent. You *do* not value intuitions, nature's work in you, as you do conclusions, of your own. They are worth as much, perhaps more; but God makes his gifts more precious to us, by engaging our powers to grasp and to realize them.

But a fifth law of progress is, that it is subject to conditions imposed upon it, by material nature. We hear much of the conquest of nature, of its subjection to human use and convenience, to human progress especially. But I suppose there is a limit somewhere. I do not know whether men will yet fly or sail through the air; but I suppose they will never fly or sail to the moon. No aeronaut expects to ascend to Saturn. But to be quite serious; would you not say as you look at the nobler part of man—and would you not feel as if you were asserting a kind of self-evident truth, when you say, that he has a right to the development and culture of his mind—a right to be educated—a right to be taught—instructed—cultivated? I think we often hear something like this. And some truth there is in the assertion; but it is not absolute, in the way that it is commonly put; it is not one of the self-evident, universal, unlimited propositions. It is controlled to a certain extent by other considerations—by obstacles, that is to say, in material nature. The mass of mankind must *labor;* and must spend the most of their lives in that way. Their right to mental culture, at least in the ordinary sense of the phrase, is subject to that condition. Perhaps they get a better training than schoolmen would give them. I believe they do. I devoutly believe in the lessons of the great taskmaster. I believe, that oftentimes men who labor in the field and the workshop—who turn their hands to this and that—who address their faculties to a thousand varying exigencies—who come into instant contact with men and things, and learn patience, perseverance, and self-denial, and in whose hand, and frame, and mind, is the might and mystery of *work*, are wiser than many who read books all the day long. Nay, there are those, to whom the printed page is for ever a sealed book, who yet are wiser, and better, and happier than the proudest philosopher that looks down upon them. Certainly I do not disparage any good learning. But it is well that we should understand—we who, as a nation, are wont to value reading, writing, and arithmetic, above all knowledge; that there is another kind of training in the great school of life; that it sets limits to book-learning, and is often better.

The last law of progress which I shall mention, springs from the *social* relation; it is the community, or rather the common dependency, of all social and political interests; it is, what is often called of late from the French writers, the solidarity of the human race; and I think there was need of the word. It comes from the Latin, *sŏlĭdus*, solid, and means that every man's interest and culture are bound in with the solid mass of all human welfare. We are all partners in a firm; and such a firm that no man living can get out of it. *My* comfort, *my* ease, facility, opportunity to cultivate my own estate or mind, cannot stand apart and alone. I may say, "What to me are the poor, the beggars, the drunken ?" But the next I know, the poor tax me, the beggar robs me, the drunken mars my plate, breaks my pitcher, or burns my house. And in higher relations—the general state of literature and science, the general state of religion—Shakspeare's Drama, Sir Walter's Fiction, Cuvier's Physiology, Augustine's, Pelagius' Creed—affect my mind, my learning, my progress. Alternately I am giver and receiver. However humble I may be, yet not a thought of mine lights upon the earth, even in casual talk, but it sinks into its bosom and brings forth fruit, or rises and wanders in the air; and like "bread cast upon the waters, returns to me after many days." I live upon the common food of human thought. I breathe through the pores of the world. I am a part of the world—bound up with it in this all-comprehending solidarity of interests.

The same thing is true in our political relations; and it deserves to be thoughtfully considered; and especially in these days—yet more especially among ourselves. A State implies a compact among its members. They agree together to do certain things, and to abstain from certain things. Deny, repudiate, nullify this compact, and the State ceases to exist. The compact, I say, is restrictive as well as permissive. The parties to it consent that their freedom, their free action, their pursuit of any object, however they may think it otherwise right or advantageous, shall be subject to this restriction. They agree to give up a portion of their natural rights, in order to create a political community. Thus, if a man lived alone upon an island—and which was his if you please by right of discovery—he might hunt, fish, plant, gather, turn the course of waters, do any thing he pleased; and these would be natural rights. But suppose that a thousand adventurers arrive at the island, and he agrees with them to form a government, to divide the land, and to assign to each one a portion, as property; then he gives up, so far, his natural rights. And so it is with all his relations to the State. He is bound in with it to certain conditions. And if he assumes the right to violate these conditions, that assumption is revolutionary, destructive, fatal. He may tell us of a progress of thought in certain respects—of rights that override the law—of the great rights of *humanity* (and it is a solemn word, to which I am bound to listen—it may be the word struggling in my own deepest heart and I will more particularly consider it soon); nevertheless, it is certain that so far as any man listens to such pleas for breaking the compact, he destroys the State. For the State—unles it be a despotism of some Louis Fourteenth, of which he is the sum and the substance—lives, and has its being, only in a constitutional compact.

I have thus attempted briefly to expound six laws of human progress—to show that it implies moral freedom and individual responsibility; that it must be experimental and gradual; and that it is subject to conditions imposed upon it by material nature and the general state of society. To sum up the matter in fewer words; nothing that fights against the laws of human nature, of material nature, and of the common dependency of man on man, can succeed.

It may be thought a great omission, that I have not mentioned the greatest happiness of the greatest number as a law. But except in so far as this is involved in the principle of solidarity, it is the *end*, and indeed the very nature of progress, rather than the law. Montesquieu, in the third book of the Spirit of Laws, makes an acute distinction between the *nature* of a government and the *principle* of a government: the former being that by which it is what it is; the latter, that upon which it acts. Now, the progress of humanity, or of a people, *is* its growing wiser, better, happier. Human rights, duties, and interests will of course be more and more recognized in such a progress. These, then, it was not my business to insist upon; for I proposed to point out the conditions or principles upon which this progress is to be made.

Let us now attempt to bring these principles to some application. It cannot always be very definite, perhaps; but it may be some guide for us, in the questions that naturally arise. What it is just and right to propose in regard to progress—what reasonable to expect; what is fit to be undertaken—what possible to be done; and how it is to be done—these certainly are matters of great practical importance.

In regard, first and generally, to the inquiry, *how* it is to be done—*how* progress is to be made—I confess that I am constrained by my convictions to call in question, I had almost said, the whole spirit of modern reform; and indeed of every other, but the Christian Reform. Let us consider it. Here is a progress to be made. That is, there is to be reform. Better things are to *be*, and to be *done;* and "better still in infinite progression." Every body admits it. Especially, at the *present day*, every body admits it. The idea of progress has taken fast hold of the modern ages, as it never did of the ancient. And, moreover, this progress, while certain, must be gradual, experimental, and blended in strict solidarity with a great mass of interests. Why then must reforms be taken up with violence? Why degenerate into partisan strifes? Why do we not calmly engage in them as if they belonged to the order of the world? It is said, I know, that all revolutions, all great changes for the better, have been violent, and probably must be so. I do not see the necessity, even in political revolutions. The Reform Bill, in England, was not a violent revolution; and most constitutional changes in England, unlike those in France, have been peaceful. But revolutions in *opinion*, have their place *exclusively* in the *mind.* They are to be carried on by writing books, not fighting battles; by the agency of clear thoughts, not furious passions. Nay, they are hindered by furious passions. The object is to change the mind of a people, to bring it over to another opinion. But violence inflames, distorts, prejudices the public mind; sets it *against* the proposed change. Violence is the atmosphere, not of truth, but of error, of falsehood, of perverted seeing. A quiet, deep-felt, earnest appeal, like the calm and penetrating sunlight, would do more to strip off the close-casing garments of old error, than all this wind of excitement.

"Fine talk!" the reformer may say,—"here is the whole mass, the whole conservatism of the world opposed to me." Is it so? I answer: that seems to me an argument for modesty. Why, I say again, therefore, this *arrogance* of reform—this outrageous assurance—this browbeating confidence, like to which there is nothing to be seen, arrayed on the side of the whole world's opinion? A man who stands up before the whole world, and says, "Give up your opinion to me, and take mine," it seems to me should, at the least, be modest. He may be zealous, he may be deeply in earnest; nay, he may be *right;* but it appears to me at the same time, that modesty becomes him, and can do neither him nor his cause any harm.

Be this as it may—and it may be a matter of taste if you please—but certainly nothing can justify the uncharitableness, the abuse, the positive detraction that mars, in so many cases, the reform movements of the day. Evil *speaking*, *false* speaking, are bad things, let the cause they espouse be ever so good. I speak plainly. It is no business nor pretension of mine to *patronize* reforms or reformers. But I certainly feel a strong interest in many of the reforms of the day. And there is not one of them, in which I do not see some good ends. And *Reformers* are the last men that I would have disappear from the world. But I demand of them, and I entreat them too, as men engaged in the noble cause of progress, that they act nobly, and speak nobly—with calmness, modesty and candor, howsoever it be with courage and earnestness. It is a pity that the cause of progress, the cause of reform in other words, which is the grand interest of the collective race of mankind—which is the very destiny of the world—should be brought under such heavy misconstruction as now lies upon it, through the faults of its most prominent advocates. Not, indeed, that the whole army of progress is to be confounded with the vanguard; but the vanguard naturally makes the first and strongest impression.

The truth is, that public sentiment, in large and influential quarters, is alienated from what is good in the reform movements of the day, by the evil that is in them. The repugnance for the most part is cold and silent, and may be the less suspected. *Mine* might be so, but I choose to speak out; because I take an interest in these movements—in and for them. I say plainly, then, physician, heal thyself; reformer, reform thyself; do not ask me to take your medicine unless it works better with you; do not ask me to go with you till you make me better like your company. If the Christian religion itself had been advocated as some of your reforms are, I should hardly have been won to it, and certainly not to its Apostles. See how nobly, candidly, charitably, tenderly, ay, and modestly, Paul pleaded for *that* Reform, and how anxious he was to keep the bond of its discipleship strong and unbroken. And he did so. But what sort of spectacle do our modern reformers present? quarrelling among themselves—splitting into parties, who assail one another as bitterly as they ever did any body else.

There *must* be something wrong here; and it is high time to ask if there cannot be something better, a new ideal of the thing, a *reform of reform* effected. It is not enough to say of any men, that they have done some good to the cause they have espoused. The true question is, have they done the most in their power, and the least evil that the case admitted? It is upon this question that the severe and enlightened judgment of after times will pronounce its verdict.

But let us proceed to consider some of the particular changes or reforms proposed. They invite our consideration. They ask in fact for our co-operation. They are really, many of them, matters of great interest. And it is not unreasonable, as it seems to me, that one should wish to say what he thinks of them, though his opinion may be of no great importance. But it is the aggregate of individual and mostly unimportant opinions, that makes up the great mass of *public* opinion; and *that* is of no little importance. Whatever, therefore, one can do to clear up his own judgment, or to help that of others, I suppose he may fitly do.

Most of those who take the trouble to address the public on what are called Reform measures, commonly do so from a strong interest, either *for* or *against* them. They are either conservatives or ultraists—either against, altogether against any proposed change, or for it to the utmost extent. Now I shall frankly tell you that I belong to neither party. It is a very unpopular profession, I know; but I ask no body's pity, and I deprecate no man's displeasure. I believe that I am here in the company of many liberal minds, who will not construe me unjustly; and I shall say nothing of the delicacy of my position—nothing of being between two fires—nothing of the unlikelihood of pleasing any body. I am not speaking, I frankly say, to please *any body*, I am speaking—just to please myself—to speak, at any rate, my own mind. Let me have, for this evening, the liberty to do this; and call it a very strange mind, if you will. I really think there may be some advantage in it. I really think that the grandest Reform Society that could be got up in this country, would be a society of people to speak their own mind, and please nobody. Our whirling eccentricities want that balance wheel. I can tell the moderatism—(if I may make the word)—the moderatism of this country, that it is asleep and dumb, just where, of all countries in the world, its voice is most needed to be heard. I say, then, for myself and for to-night, that I belong to *no* party. With regard to conservatism and ultraism, as the general division of opinion, running through all other questions and ranging men into parties—I am, in some views, a conservative. I profess to venerate the past. I value the results of past experience. I think they are to be parted from with great caution. I think it is monstrous for an individual man to stand up against the collected experience of the world and say, "it is nought—it is nonsense." I have a sort of reverence for what the whole race of my fellows have come to think and feel, after a trial and progress of six thousand years. I do not believe that the stream which has flowed so far is a miserable puddle, or black as Styx and Acheron. And whoever says that—whoever says, "away with the past! let us have a new world to-day!"—whoever, forgetting that all good changes must be gradual and slowly wrought out, proposes to carry a people at once from absolutism and ignorance into the largest liberty and suffrage, or rashly to transfer woman from her accustomed sphere to seats in the Legislature and the Cabinet, seems to me to have fallen into the madness of reaction against old abuses. And yet, on the other hand, the conservatism that desires to hold all fast where it is—that is prejudiced and set against all changes, all reforms—that for ever says, "let things alone; they are very well"—why, it is a conservation that would stop the progress, and quench the hope, and challenge the very destiny of the world.

But let us go, as I proposed, to some of the special reforms.

And, first, to that which is so called, and which is advocated by some, though I believe not by many, of the gentler sex, under the name of "Woman's Rights." Now, I should not wonder if the very terms of this statement should be partly displeasing to two sorts of persons. Some *women* might not choose that theirs should be called "the gentler sex,"—and certainly the appellation is not very likely to be given to such recusants—they say that their just claims are always compromised by this apparent courtesy. And it may offend some strong conservative *men*, that this subject should be seriously mentioned at all—that it should, so to speak, be tabled for discussion. But I stick to my point. I am neither a conservative nor an ultraist. I have always felt that woman has suffered great wrongs, not only among Indians and profligates, but in what is called our better modern civilization. It is not affection alone, not chivalry, not homage only, that woman demands—things easy to pay—but *justice;* a just sense of the true relations of mind to mind, of one human being to another. The right that lies in might, the right of the strong, is always a suspicious thing, dangerous to exercise, liable in fact to unintentional and unconscious abuse. I think that a man of just and delicate feeling will always watch himself on this point. I believe that, from the ordinary construction of the *marriage* tie, there is by coarse, uncultivated minds, an immense deal of wrong inflicted—of injustice, hardship, and cruelty endured; and that, even by better and more refined persons, woman is often deprived of the independence of character, the freedom to think and act for herself, to which she is entitled. Before God these parties are equal souls, with equal rights, though circumstances may make a difference; and I would never insert, in the marriage service, the word *obey* for woman; though, in ordinary cases of difference, if it comes to that, it would be, I think, her duty and her wisdom to yield her opinion. Yet I do not like the word *obey*, and should never desire a woman to use it to me; and, indeed, in the existing state of society, I have thought it the dictate of a just moral policy, as well as of true courtesy, to omit it. It *was* necessary,

I suppose, in the ruder age, in which the Apostle Paul wrote, to lay down so definite a precept as "wives obey your husbands," but it does not appear to me necessary or useful now.

I said that circumstances make a difference; and I mean a difference of pursuits between man and woman. Thus, I think, that the prosecution of business naturally belongs to the former—therefore the care of property—therefore some superior control of it. But, it does not follow that the ascendency should be so complete and irresponsible as it is. The wife may be a silent partner in the concern; but she ought to be regarded as a partner more than she is, and there ought to be more checks upon the power of an improvident husband to waste the property she brings into the partnership. And I protest altogether against the power of a drunken husband to take his wife's *earnings* to squander upon his vices; but yet I doubt whether, in general, *two equal property-holders in a family* would not breed more difficulty than it would relieve.

As to education—let every human being be educated—let every human mind be expanded as much as possible. The theory of an essential difference of intellectual powers in the sexes, of any other difference than circumstances make, is, in my view, too absurd to be considered.

So far I go; but here I must stop—and stop short. When it is contended, that women should do business, labor out of doors as men do—should vote, appear in public life, hold office, be members of Congress, Cabinet Ministers, Presidents—and why not Captains and Commodores, as well?—I will not say what madness! though that is my feeling; but, I say, the laws of progress, the nature of persons, the relations to the material world, the relations to the social body, forbid. I believe, indeed, that there is a constitutional difference between the sexes, which destines the one to out-of-door life, and the other to in-door life. If it be not so, I should like to have some one tell me, why the one has a *beard* and the other not. But if this be thought to be trifling with the subject; or, if the idea of such constitutional difference be said to be a matter of vague sentiment, then I point to palpable facts. Who must bear and nurse children? Who then must tend them? Who then must stay beneath the domestic roof? And which sex acquires, from these causes, a delicacy of frame and fibre unknown to the other? Can women go out to work—hunt, fish, fell trees, quarry stone, build houses—as well as the men? Can they leave their little charge at home, and go into the courts, to Congress, to the camp? Deliver us from a Congress of *men* and *women!* Our politics are vexed and perplexed enough already. What they would be with that element of female fascination, impulse, and sensitiveness flung into them, were hard to say or imagine; but a burning house, with the most delicate and volatile oil flung upon it, might give one an idea.

Turn, now, to another social question—that between the *family* and the *phalanstery*. The great argument for the latter is, that it would free the world from much of its ignorance, pauperism, misery. Men living in community, it is said, would relieve one another's labor—enlighten, cheer, help one another. Those dark pools of physical and moral degradation opened, especially in our cities, into which the poor, the indolent, the imbecile, the reckless, are falling year after year—the horror and almost the despair of good men—would be cleansed and cleared out. I must doubt it.

The most powerful preservative, perhaps, in the world, from indolence, improvidence and degradation, is individual responsibility. It seems to me an indispensable law of progress. You take that away, or you essentially weaken it, in the phalanstery. Every man, then, is to be fed, and clothed, and housed, and made tolerably comfortable, let him do as he will. Or, if not; if you drive him away because he will not work, you make him more poor and miserable than he was before, and a desperate outcast and marauder into the bargain; and, moreover, you give up the phalanstery principle.

For myself, I certainly should not like to live in a phalanstery. I must say, I should very much rather not; but I should yet more fear its influence, *i. e.* upon the moral *freedom* of men. *Epidemics* there would be bad enough; but I should dread, still more, epidemics in the mind — the infection of example. When, in the theological school, we heard a young man declaim, we always knew what college he came from. When I passed through Germany, I saw a great many villages, every house in which was built like every other; there was a ruling fashion in building, which, it seemed, nobody could depart from. I should be afraid men's minds, in a phalanstery, would be like those houses. I should distrust such a mechanism. The disparity, the conflict of minds, is the very nurture of truth and means of progress. These schools of human device will never compete successfully with that great school which God has opened, when "He set the solitary" not in phalansteries, but "in families."

Let us now turn to forms of *human violence*, and inquire wherein, and how far, and how fast, they can be stayed? I would to God the time might come, when not one drop of human blood shall stain the earth, by the hand of executioner or soldier! But there are some things that are fast fixed in human nature—for that nature is one of our laws—fast fixed in human nature, and are not easily or quickly to be removed. A man stands before me—a good and innocent man—and against him comes, in open day, or steals upon him with stealthy step, a monster in human shape, and murders him before my eyes. My feeling cries out—all human feeling, from the beginning of the world, cries out—"Thy blood ought to pay for that accursed act!" Now, I am not to be reasoned out of this feeling by any theory of punishment being inflicted solely as an example, or for the good of society. That *is* one *object* of punishment, but not its special significance. The murderer *ought to suffer adequately for what he has done*; and if he himself were immediately inspired with the right feeling, he would say, "Take my life for his. I demand it." This sense of justice, I say, is not to be ignored, or scorned, or scandalized, as unchristian. And it is very poor jesting to propose, that the man or the minister of religion who takes this ground, should himself become the hangman.

Can justice, in this matter, yield to mercy? Can a milder punishment be safely substituted? I do not know. I would to Heaven it might! But this I know: that any reasoning—call it mild, merciful, Christian-like, or what you will—that takes out the element of righteous justice from the penalty, takes out the very essence and heart of the law, and makes it a mere trick to awe the world to virtue.

I look for better times. I hope the day will come

when some other punishment may be substituted for that awful execution, that stops, at once and for ever, the current of life. But I believe that the time will *never* come, when he who sheddeth man's blood will not *deserve* that by man his blood shall be shed. And if he deserves that, does he not deserve the lesser punishment which mercy proposes to inflict? And is the solemn sense of justice to be denied and cast out of the penalty? If it were, mercy itself would have no meaning.

And so with regard to war. Who will not hope that the horrible custom is to be done away? It cannot stand for ever, if there is to be a progress in the world. Barbarous trial of brute strength—for that is what it is—brute strength brought in to settle the claims of nations; a game of kings and rulers, where the people are always losers; a waster of treasure and life, slaying thousands and ten thousands; a payment of blood and tears to buy desolation and misery; —if there is common sense in the world, and civilization is not a name, and progress a dream, this must come to an end.

But it must come to an end because of the very enormity of the thing. Not every fine-spun argument against it, is sound and strong; not every proposition made for its abolition, is rational and wise. To deny us all right to defend ourselves against violence and wrong, or to take life in any case, or to keep arms and munitions for our protection—such dialectics, to my mind, do not help the good cause. But let the horribleness of the thing be shown and be insisted on—be portrayed in all its hatefulness and atrocity, till men shall feel that they can bear it no longer.

And now let us come to the great and terrible

question of *slavery*. In the survey which I am taking of certain questions, this, the greatest of all, cannot be omitted; and on this subject let me say, I still adhere to my position. I am not an ultraist. I have, to a certain extent, sympathies with both the parties to this question; I respect the feelings and situation of the people of the South; I share the sentiments of the bulk of the people at the North. And as I have had the fortune to be misconstrued on this subject, I am still more desirous to use the privilege which I have craved this evening, of speaking for myself.

In a speech which I made in Pittsfield last winter, and also in a lecture which I delivered in Boston, I did not discuss the present fugitive slave law, though I was immediately represented as a violent advocate for it, but rather addressed myself to the question whether we at the North could, in conscience, yield our assent to *any* such bill—to *any* bill that should give the Southern master the power to reclaim one of his slaves that had fled to us for refuge. Should we make our Northern cities "cities of refuge" to the fugitive; or should we say to him, "Under the circumstances, we do not think it right to offer you an asylum and protection?" *That* was the question. Were we bound by the highest obligations of conscience and humanity to say to the master, "You shall not have your slave; we will not hear of rendition; we will have no law about it, any way?" The abolitionists themselves might have seen in that speech the painful struggle of a conscience to decide, not whether this (to them so odious) law could be obeyed, but whether any law of the kind could be obeyed. After the publication of that speech, I received a letter from a friend, saying, "Your speech has been read among us with much satisfaction; even the greatest of our abolitionists has nothing to say against it, but that you ought to have denounced the present bill." I replied, "Tell my friend, that of the two I am the greater abolitionist; for I so detest *all* fugitive slave bills, that I have hardly patience to go into detail and discrimination—to say which is better and which is worse."

But I did not denounce the bill for other reasons. I felt hardly competent to do so. It had been framed by the supreme legislature of the land; and whether it was constitutional, whether it was the best law that could be made, I was not prepared to say. Besides, when the tide of public opinion was running so strong against the law, as to threaten, in my opinion, to break down the barriers of the Constitution and the Union, I did not think it right to join the malcontents in decrying the law. Moreover, I wished to put the question at once upon its ultimate merits. The main offence does not lie in *this* law, but in *any* effective law. As I said in my speech—"The abolitionists ought themselves to see that they will never be satisfied. I myself feel that no bill can ever be framed that will not be distasteful to me."

I am sensible that this language cannot be agreeable to the people of the South. I am, doubtless, a very bad controversialist, being of no side, saying what I think, without proposing to satisfy any party—thinking, indeed, that in this fearful debate there is something right on both sides. But this, at least, must be plainly said: *Nothing* can make a fugitive slave bill palatable to us at the North; if we submit to any such law, it is the most reluctant concession to a sense of duty. All men, North and South, may easily understand that. The people of the South should take no offence at it; it is what they themselves would feel, in a change of circumstances. If a fugitive Russian serf or Algerine captive were seized in the streets of Charleston, to be borne back to bondage, every humane and high-minded man there would behold the spectacle with pain and indignation. And if a man, albeit of a different color and lineage from my own, yet a *man*, and a man, too, perhaps, who had lived ten years here by my side, and had done me kindly offices,—if such a man were caught before my door by the Southern emissary, and manacled, to be remanded to slavery, my tears would start and my blood would boil with indignation and pity at the sight.

It is a spectacle wounding to humanity. As between the master and the slave, it is the infliction of a great wrong. It may be our duty not to interfere—we cannot immediately right all wrongs in the world; and this is one; but it is not our duty to suppress the feelings of justice and humanity that arise in our bosoms. The people of the South should understand this; and it much concerns them to understand it. For they have essentially hurt their position before the world, by demanding this new law. They had better, in my opinion, have left things as they were—left the law to stand as an acknowledgment of their constitutional right—but at the same time, let it fall into desuetude. They recover a few slaves—a very few; but they outrage the sentiments of all mankind. They do not *want* among them the men whom they recapture—certain as these men are, when carried back, to spread disaffection among their people—likely also to be persons of a *better class* among their slaves, and more fit for freedom. They had better let them go. As I have known slaveholders to *say*, "If one of our slaves escapes, we shall not pursue him; he has a natural right to be free; if he makes that perilous struggle for freedom, let him have it; the *most* of our people do not wish to leave us; they are sensible that they are not qualified to take care of themselves; let things remain in this way; we must accept the good and evil of our condition, and make the best of it."

Still it would be wrong for us to interfere between the master and slave, with any other force than that of argument. We have promised that we would not do so. It is a part of our national compact. Our Union was founded, in part, upon that agreement. No Union can stand without it. And if we break the compact in behalf of *fugitive* slaves, *why not as well in behalf of the rest?* Yet the abolitionists themselves disclaim any intention, by force or law, to touch the body of slaves in actual possession of their masters. But why *not?* One man stands on one side of a State line, and is a fugitive; another stands ten feet or ten miles from him on the other side, and is in the hands of his master. Can a few feet, or a few miles, make any difference in the *principle* that justifies interference? I press the question. Why do not the abolitionists make a crusade upon the South to deliver the slave? Is it because we have made a compact with the Southern States to leave their slaves in their possession? But so have we made a compact not to withhold, but to surrender the fugitive. I say again—why do they not make a slave-delivering crusade? Is it because of the evil, and mischief, and peril that it would involve? Then I say that the same argument should restrain them from interfering to rescue the fugitive.

But *here*, it will be said, is the point where the *question of conscience* presses: "The fugitive has a right to be free; if you help the master to catch and hold him, you *violate* his right; and it is a *sin* before Heaven." I answer, that the compact does *not* bind me, and no bill formed in compliance with it ought to bind me, to do any such thing. "What!" it may be said, "do not the constable, and the commissioner, and the bystanders lend their aid—do *they* not catch, and hold, and enslave the man?" I answer, no. By the laws of this government, the man is a slave before they touch him; and no action can *make* him to be that which he *is*. But suppose it were otherwise. Suppose that South Carolina were a foreign State, and that we had made a convention with her, in the very words of our Constitution. What *is* that bond? Not to catch, hold, or enslave her people that flee from her, but simply to "*deliver them up*"—simply not to withhold them. "What is the meaning, then," it will be asked, "of the legal process that precedes this delivery?" I understand it to be this. We will not let irresponsible persons come into our territory and seize whom they will, and bear him off to bondage. If you claim any man as owing you service, you must prove that he *is* the man you say he is, and not another. You must prove this, according to the forms of law. The *legal* marshal shall take him—before the *legal* commissioner; his case shall be *legally* examined; and then, if he is given up to his master, we simply promise you that there shall be no rescue with the strong hand; civil order and the course of the law shall be protected, though the *posse comitatus* be called out for the purpose. I repeat it; the bill does *not* make us slave-catchers. The Southern master, or his agent, lays his hand upon a colored man here at the North, and says, "This is one of my people, and he must come with me."

The bill says, "Stop; you must not take this man as one of your people till you have *proved* that he is such. *I* lay my hand on him to *protect* him, till you have established this fact. If you make out your case, then the Northern citizen is bound by the Constitution and the law of the land not to interfere in the matter. The master may take his slave—it is his own affair. And if there shall be any attempt at rescue, the bystanders are required, as they are in all cases of resistance and violence, to sustain the law and the public order."

The point here involved is, doubtless, most material. I firmly deny that it was ever meant by the Constitution that we should assist the master to catch or carry back his slave. The language of the instrument is, that he "shall be *delivered up*." This phrase very naturally expresses what would follow as the result of the civil process, supposing the claim to be made out. The fugitive is in the hands of the Court—of the legal authority appointed to decide upon his case. The Court "delivers him up"—*i. e.*, it simply says to the claimant, "you may take him." The action of the Court is not aid, nor assistance, nor approval, nor sympathy with the claimant; but simple rendition. "Delivering up" a slave, like "delivering up" a criminal or a man charged with crime, is not constituting ourselves judges of his case; but it is simply saying to a neighboring sovereignty, "we leave him to you; we do not interfere to protect the fugitive."

Indeed, the real offence in this matter seems to lie in the re-enactment of this law at all, and not in the terms of the present bill. There was no trial by jury *before*, no writ of *habeas corpus*. The Court now constituted is as *respectable*, the investigation as *ample* as before. There is no serious danger, and no sincere apprehension that free men—*i. e.*, men by birth or purchase free—will be remanded to slavery. There is no reason to think that many persons will be reclaimed any way. I do not believe that ten persons have been recovered, or that twenty ever will be. The real offence, I repeat, lies in the re-enactment of the law. I believe it is felt by many, in this country and in England, that it is a base subserviency to Southern threats, or a sacrifice of principle to policy. I do not so regard it. I believe it was right thus to re-assure the Southern States, since they required the re-assurance, that we did not mean to interfere with their system, nor to violate the compact of the Constitution. And if we did not and do not mean to do this; if we do not mean to open an asylum for Southern slaves in the North, then it was not unmeet to make a declaration that should prevent them from seeking it; and such I understand really to be the main purpose and effect of this Fugitive Slave Bill. It will not be the means, perhaps, of apprehending twenty slaves; but it will probably prevent hundreds from coming here. And if we do not mean to have them come here, nor to hold out any lure to them; if we do not think that *this is the way to avert from the nation a great and overshadowing peril*, it is proper that we should say so.

In truth, as it seems to me, it only needs that a man, instead of indulging in vague, and it may be, eloquent declamation, should take some decided ground on this subject, to be brought to a right conclusion. What do you *say?* I ask. Would you, as the member of a national sovereignty, American or English, propose rudely to violate one of the written bonds of your Constitution? *Do* you, as an American citizen, mean to say to the Southern States, "We will break our covenant with *you*, come what may. We will not wait to reason; we will not wait for any legal modification; we will break the bond to-day." You do not, you never did, say that. There has been a Fugitive Slave Law in existence all along; you never took any such ground with regard to it. Well, then, if you do not propose to overthrow the Constitution and break up the Union, you must acquiesce in some kind of Fugitive Slave Law. And it is in vain to say that the present law is so much worse than the former, as to justify a resistance now, which you never thought of before. In fact it is not worse, but better, for the slave than the former.

The declamation on this subject may be eloquent; I have received letters from gentlemen, both at home and abroad, full of eloquent expostulation, full of beautiful pleas for humanity. I sympathize with those pleas. I would make the case of every man—American, English, or African—my own. If there be wrongs, if there be stripes, if there be sorrows in the world, I would feel them as if they were inflicted upon myself. And I must take simple leave to say, that I see nothing in the *humanity* of Abolition writers and speakers that makes me feel that I must humble myself in its presence. Sorrows and wrongs enough there are in the very structure of society, and we must struggle out of them as well as we can. But when that fathomless abyss of calamities and sorrows is opened to me, that would be made by the sundering of our national bond, I must pause, I must deliberate, I must consider with anxious and painful care what is my duty; and that is what I have endeavored to do.

I say I must consider. I must consider the great

bond of the Union, which we must not break; and I must consider the rights of the fugitive too. Liberty *is* his own proper right; and I believe that every slave-master feels it—feels that he *himself* would escape, if he could, in similar circumstances. It is the very impulse of humanity to do so. I can conceive, indeed, of a higher thing than this impulse. I may be *reminded* of the case of Socrates bowing to the majesty of the Athenian law, and *refusing* to escape; and I admire the conduct of Socrates. And I only say, show me the *slave*-man who, for the sake of the public order and law, is disposed to do the same thing, and I will admire *him;* but for *me* to compel him to do it, is quite another thing. I say I would *admire* him. I said, in my speech, "I would consent that my own brother"—for certainly I was never guilty of the vulgar irreverence of thus alluding to a more venerable relative; and those who have frequently asserted it, must settle the account with their truth and decency as they can--*this* is what I said, both in my speech and lecture: "I would consent"—for I said nothing of *sending* any body—"I would *consent* that my own brother, my own son, should go (*i. e.* into slavery)—*ten times rather* would I go myself—than that this Union should be sacrificed for me or for us;" and I am ready to stand by this as a just and honorable sentiment; and I can only wonder that any man should think it extravagant or ridiculous. Indeed, I suppose the only chance of making it appear so, was to connect with it the falsehood to which I have just referred.

And now let me add, that in all this I place myself on the ground of moral conviction, as truly so as any abolitionist in the world. *Conscience—conscience*

—must I repeat it?—*conscience* is the ground on which I stand. Continually is it said or implied by the Abolitionists and their sympathizers, that *they* look to conscience for their law, and *we* to the State, or to State expediency. No; *this* rather, in my view, is the difference. *They* take the bare instinct of conscience for their guide—we profess to take the wisdom of conscience for ours; they take *one* view of the matter—we are obliged to take *many*. There is an important distinction here, which it seems to me is constantly overlooked. The principle of conscience is one thing—the application of the principle is another thing. The former may be right—the latter entirely wrong. What great moral mistake was there ever in the world, that has not sheltered itself, and that honestly, under the plea of conscience! Religious intolerance, political proscription, wild fanaticism, "wrath, malice, and all uncharitableness," have ever had that plea. Conscience is no more exempt from aberration than any other principle. Its very elevation may be an exposure. It derives from Heaven, and will not hear of earth-born question or doubt. It stands so high, that it cannot *see* the plain paths of duty that lie around it. It is self-confident in the same proportion. It is blinded—by excess of light. It is made giddy—by the pure air of abstractions. It sins the more—through the assurance of being right. It is guilty of inhumanity, for the same reason that Paul was, because it verily thinks that it is doing God service. How much of the hard censure, cruel defamation, and moral ruffianism, that we see to-day, has its origin in this instinct of conscience! Men were not made to be governed by instincts, however holy, but by reason, also—by reflection—by circumstances—by the *right*, indeed, but also by the universal welfare, which is ever coincident with the right.

Upon the ground of a reflective conscience, therefore, I endeavor to place myself; and these points are very clear to me.

Firstly: That the immediate emancipation of the Southern slaves would not be right; they are not prepared for freedom, nor do they generally desire it.

Secondly: That till this event takes place, it would be fatal to that order of things, fatal to our peace and Union, for us to hold them free and irreclaimable, the moment they touch our soil.

Thirdly: That, therefore, there *must* be some kind of fugitive slave law.

And Fourthly: That the present law is not more stringent than its predecessor; that it contains no new features of intolerable tyranny, such that it must be rejected on this account; that it is *not* rejected on this account, but because *any* effective bill would be disliked and resisted.

Alas! the tide is sweeping on like fate, bearing on its bosom untold calamities and perils. In 40 years, it is estimated that there will be nine millions of slaves in the Southern States; the worn-out land will not be able to bear them, nor their impoverished masters to keep them. Horrible convulsions must ensue—civil or servile wars. Something, then, must be done, and soon done, to avert the catastrophe. The nation must put forth its strength; North and South must put brotherly shoulders to the work; especially does all original motive power to help, lie with our brethren in the South. And yet we spend all this dread interval in mutual recrimination! instead of devising ways of relief, we devise stumbling-blocks. It is the pleasure of many at the South to represent us as ferocious and selfish fanatics; and of many at the North to heap opprobrium and indignity upon men as kind, and generous, and honorable, and conscientious as ourselves. One thing, at least, is perfectly plain to me: that nothing but moderation on all sides—nothing but a calmness and brotherly kindness such as we have not yet seen, can conduct us out of these perils—can solve for our country this tremendous problem.

www.ingramcontent.com/pod-product-compliance
Lightning Source LLC
LaVergne TN
LVHW011123110826
845150LV00008B/2235

* 9 7 8 1 4 1 8 1 9 5 3 7 3 *